CRIMSON TOPAZ
(South America)

LARGE
TREE NYMPH
(Asia)

CAIRNS
BIRDWING
(New Guinea
to Australia)

BLUE
MORPHO
(South
America)

TIGER
SWALLOWTAIL
(North America)

BEE
HUMMINGBIRD
(Cuba)

LODDIGE'S
RAQUET-TAIL
(Peru)

TIGER PIERID
(Central/South America ·
Mexico · West Indies)

CRAMER'S MESENE
(Central/South
America)

GRANT'S ZEBRA
(Africa)

ALIKI
My Visit to the Zoo

MARABOU STORK
(Africa)

OSTRICH
(Africa)

HarperCollinsPublishers

This book is dedicated to the magnificent animals in the world and to those who help them survive.

Grateful thanks to many people for their help, advice, patience, and generosity. Here are some of them:
Robin Dalton *(Queens Wildlife Center)*,
Gail Eaton and Sheila Wilson *(Atlanta Zoo)*,
Georgeanne Irvine *(San Diego Zoo)*, Joel Edelstein *(San Diego Wild Animal Park)*, Susan Biggs *(National Zoological Park)*,
Antoinette S. Maciolek and Derrick Boskie *(Philadelphia Zoological Park)*, Linda Corcoran *(Bronx Zoo)*, Franz Brandenberg,
Kate M. Jackson, Barbara Fenton, Elynn Cohen, Virginia Anagnos,
Tim Hamilton, Joanna and Alfred Uhry, Emily K. Hachett,
Robert and Judith Waldman, Helen and Vasilios Lambros,
Minerva Theodos, Ann Liacouras, Antoinette Gianopulos,
and especially—thanks to Liza Baker, guardian angel.

The zoo in this book has been created from several existing zoos. The illustrations were prepared with blood, sweat, tears, sleepless nights, grueling determination, a pain in the neck, and the will to survive.

Library of Congress Cataloging-in-Publication Data   Aliki.   My visit to the zoo / Aliki.   p.   cm.
Summary: A day at the zoo introduces the different animals that exist in the world, where they come from, what their natural habitats are like, whether or not they are endangered, and the role zoos and conservation parks play today.
ISBN 0-06-024939-0.— ISBN 0-06-024943-9 (lib. bdg.) — ISBN 0-06-446217-X (pbk.)
1. Zoo animals—Juvenile literature.   2. Zoos—Juvenile literature.   [1.Zoo animals.   2. Zoos.]
I. Title.   QL77.5.A43   1997 96-9897   590'.74'4—dc20   CIP AC   Typography by Elynn Cohen
For information address HarperCollins Children's Books, a division of HarperCollins Publishers,
10 East 53rd Street, New York, NY 10022.
Visit us on the World Wide Web! http://www.harperchildrens.com
10 11 12 13 SCP 10

I didn't really want to visit the zoo.
I had been to one that made me feel sad.
The animals cramped in small, empty cages had looked sad, too.
But my cousin said this zoo was different.
So I came along and had the surprise of my life.

This zoo was like a rambling park with trees and lakes.
There were houses where the animals could sleep and eat,
and outdoor habitats where they roamed free, as they
would in the wild.
Animals from all over the world were here in one zoo.
We laughed as we planned our route on the map.
I told my cousin it was like a walk through geography.

FLAMINGO
(South America · Caribbean ·
Africa · Europe · Asia)

*Flamingos like to be in big groups.
In nature, they live and breed
in flocks of thousands.*

A flock of flamingos greeted us on our way to the Primate House.
There, all kinds of apes and monkeys entertained us outside and inside.
We heard the gibbons' loud call even before we saw them.

GIBBON
(Asia)

The gibbon leaps and swings like a gymnast.
It has long arms and grasps with its hands and feet.
You can tell a gibbon is an ape because apes have no tails.

SPIDER MONKEY
(Central/South America)

Most monkeys have tails.
The spider monkey's tail is long and prehensile—
it can grasp like a hand.

LION-TAILED MACAQUE
(southern India)

Other monkeys have nonprehensile tails,
like the friendly macaques that inspected us.
The frisky monkeylike lemur was too busy to notice.

RING-TAILED LEMUR
(Madagascar)

OLIVE BABOON
(Africa)

Big baboons live on the ground in rough, rocky places.
They walk on all fours and carry their young ones piggyback.

COLOBUS MONKEY
(Africa)

Colobus monkeys live high up in trees
and eat leaves nonstop.

Pygmy marmosets are so small,
one could fit in my pocket.
They scrape away at trees
with their sharp little teeth, and sip the sap.

PYGMY MARMOSET
(South America)

Monkeys live around the world.
New World monkeys are from South and Central America.
Old World monkeys are from Asia and Africa.
You can tell where a monkey comes from by its nose.

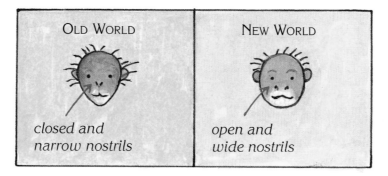

OLD WORLD

NEW WORLD

closed and
narrow nostrils

open and
wide nostrils

TOUCAN

SCARLET IBIS

PARROT

We went into the misty tropical rain forest where many primates live.
It was muggy, and noisy with the clamor of nature sounds—
birds, insects, frogs, and flowing water.
I closed my eyes and listened.

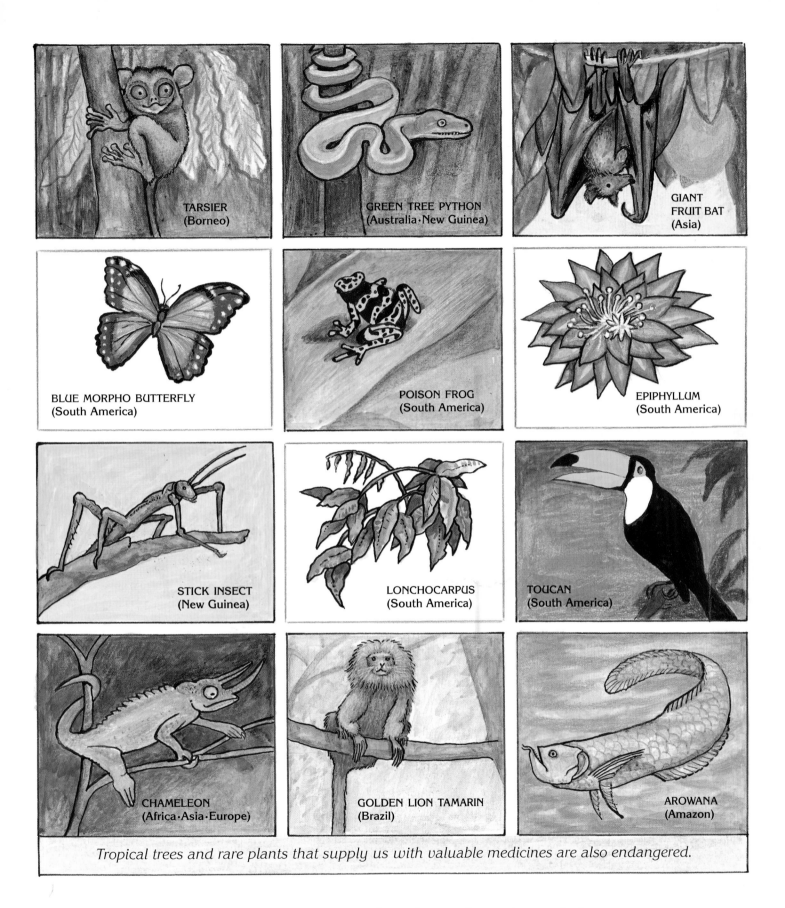

TARSIER
(Borneo)

GREEN TREE PYTHON
(Australia·New Guinea)

GIANT
FRUIT BAT
(Asia)

BLUE MORPHO BUTTERFLY
(South America)

POISON FROG
(South America)

EPIPHYLLUM
(South America)

STICK INSECT
(New Guinea)

LONCHOCARPUS
(South America)

TOUCAN
(South America)

CHAMELEON
(Africa·Asia·Europe)

GOLDEN LION TAMARIN
(Brazil)

AROWANA
(Amazon)

Tropical trees and rare plants that supply us with valuable medicines are also endangered.

Half of all wildlife species on the planet thrive in such forests.
Both animals and people are left homeless and without food
when their trees are cut down and their habitats are destroyed.

Volunteers called docents were everywhere to answer our questions.
One told us that last year this zoo celebrated a thousand births!

We found out that many animals endangered in the wild
are bred in zoos to prevent species from dying out.
Then, when a safe environment is found, they are set free.
The golden lion tamarin was nearly extinct.
Now, dozens that were raised in captivity survive in the wild.

Over at the Great Apes, everyone was looking through a window, laughing.
Apes are so like people, they are fun to watch.
The chimpanzee is the most curious and intelligent of all.
Families of chimps played and groomed each other affectionately,
and dug for honey and seeds their keeper had hidden for them.

CHIMPANZEE
(Africa)

Keepers don't feed animals directly. They hide food in places where the animals must dig, hunt, or reach for it as they would in the wild.

ORANGUTAN
(Asia)

The big long-haired orangutan likes to be up high.
It lives in treetops, wandering miles to fill up on fruit.
Here, too, orangs travel high on their new home of cables and towers.
They are loners in the wild, but friendly in captivity.
And they have fun even when they come down to take a drink.

LOWLAND GORILLA
(Africa)

A troop of busy gorillas watched us as we watched them
romp with their zoo-born twins in their jungle habitat.
Apes and other animals have been studied in the wild where they live.
That is how we know so much about them and their environment.

CHEETAH
(South Africa)

SIBERIAN TIGER
(Asia)

We went from the Great Apes to the Great Cats!
Cats have the sharp teeth of carnivores, and beautiful coats,
for which too many have been hunted.
The cheetah was quiet, but when it runs, it is the fastest cat.
The tiger is the biggest.
It stalks silently through the forest, hunting alone.
Unlike other cats, it likes to splash in streams.

16

SNOW LEOPARD
(central Asia)

LION
(Africa·Asia)

LIONESS and LION CUB
(Africa·Asia)

In nature, the rare snow leopard climbs icy mountains with its padded paws.
Here, one climbed ledges and hunted for food hidden in nooks.
At night, it sleeps in a cage built into a cool hill.

A lioness played with her cub as a lion dozed on a nearby rock.
Lions like hot weather, so when it's cold, the rock is heated.
Other big cats were resting or asleep, too.
That's how they spend most of their time—just like my little cat at home.

We rode the monorail around the open plains where many of the big cats live.
There is plenty of space for other animals and birds, too.
A flightless ostrich—the biggest of all birds—ran past.
We saw herds of grazers—zebra, antelope, and gazelle.
They all have hooves and sturdy legs, and are fast runners.

OSTRICH
(Africa)

KUDU
(South
Africa)

DORCAS GAZELLE
(Africa·Asia)

ARABIAN ORYX
(Asia)

GRÉVY'S ZEBRA
(Africa)

The tall giraffes are the lookouts of the herds, and fast runners, too.
One reached leaves tucked in a "browse tree" while Baby waited.

MARABOU STORK
(Africa)

GIRAFFE
(Africa)

OKAPI
(Africa)

In a separate enclosure was a rare forest giraffe
with a short neck—the shy okapi.

The only hungry wild animals we fed were ourselves.
Every other animal has its own special diet prepared by a nutritionist.
Each animal has its own keeper who feeds it and looks after it.
As we ate, I thought about feeding thousands of mouths a day.
Imagine ordering and preparing tons of food morning, noon, and night.
Imagine the awesome shopping bill!

Elephants love baths. Afterward, they roll in sand to protect their sensitive skin from the sun. The keeper trains the elephants to keep them active and alert.

AFRICAN ELEPHANT
(Africa)

ASIAN ELEPHANT
(Asia)

Everyone loved the playful, affectionate elephants—
especially the baby guarded by its mother.
The African elephant is the biggest land mammal,
with large ears that are the same shape as Africa.
In the wild, these elephants are endangered by poachers,
who hunt them illegally for their long ivory tusks.
The Asian elephant is rounder and smaller.

21

WHITE RHINOCEROS
(Africa)

Close by was the thick-skinned rhinoceros, hunted to near
extinction for its long horns—safe here in the zoo.

Then I saw my first meerkats—my cousin's favorites.
They would dig a fast hole, burrow in, climb out, and stand
like guards with those serious dark eyes.
I wanted to take one home, but I took a picture instead.

MEERKAT
(South Africa)

Down a steep canyon, we saw slippery seals and frisky otters,
and were even in time for the sea lion show.
All these graceful swimmers are fun to watch.

SEAL

SEA LION

OTTER

HIPPOPOTAMUS
(Africa)

You would think a 6,000-pound hippopotamus might sink, but it swims, too.
It spends much of its day sleeping in water.
At night, it wakes up and wallows around eating grass.
Whoa, Hippo! What a big mouth you have.

KOALA
(Australia)

RED KANGAROO
(Australia)

*Koalas are nocturnal. They live in eucalyptus trees, eating leaves at night.
Then they nestle down on a branch and sleep all day.*

I thought a koala was a bear, but it is a marsupial.
The mother has a pouch where her tiny newborn baby stays
until it has grown big and strong.
The kangaroo is a marsupial, too.
It bounces around on strong hind legs, like a wind-up toy—
joey and all. A joey is what a baby kangaroo is called.

GRIZZLY BEAR
(North America · Europe ·
Asia · Africa)

POLAR BEAR
(circumpolar)

Down the Bear Path, everyone was asleep
except the long-clawed grizzly
and the polar bear cuddling her cub.

GIANT PANDA
(China)

Unlike other animals, pandas have not bred successfully in captivity so far.

There are very few giant pandas in captivity, and they are endangered in the wild.
They eat mostly bamboo, and their bamboo forests are disappearing
as people move close to their habitats.

We saw birds everywhere—birds flying free in aviaries,

SPOTTED DOVE
(China)

SNOWY OWL
(circumpolar)

LORIKEET
(Australia)

birds in the Bird House, birds we could feed nectar to,

FISH EAGLE
(Africa)

CALIFORNIA CONDOR
(North America)

*It takes patience to train a bird to obey commands.
We saw how birds of prey—carnivores with huge wings—
swoop down from high places where they live.*

*The condor was saved
from extinction by
successful breeding.*

and many trained birds in the bird show.

There were tiny birds, plumed birds, songbirds, "talking" birds,

HUMMINGBIRD
(South America)

GRAY PARROT
(Africa)

MACAW
(South America)

Talking birds mimic words and other sounds perfectly.

squawking birds, a funny rumpled bird,

BIRD OF PARADISE
(New Guinea)

TAWNY FROGMOUTH
(Australia)

KINGFISHER
(worldwide)

GOLDEN-BREASTED STARLING
(Africa)

KOOKABURRA
(Australia)

and even a kookaburra sitting in an old gum tree laughing.

RED-EARED TURTLES
(North/Central/South America)

GREAT BLUE HERON
(North America)

RED-CRESTED POCHARD
(Asia·Europe)

MUTE SWAN
(Europe·Asia·North America)

EGRET
(worldwide)

We stopped to watch waterbirds, and turtles sunning piggyback on a log.
Nearby, a waterfall flowed with recycled water.
Nothing is wasted at the zoo.
Paper, plastic, glass, and cans are recycled,
and there is not a straw or balloon in sight.
They are dangerous to wildlife if they are accidently swallowed.

In the Reptile House, there were harmless snakes, venomous snakes,

CALIFORNIA MOUNTAIN KINGSNAKE
(North America)

RUSSELL'S VIPER
(Asia)

the world's biggest tortoise, which can live a hundred years,

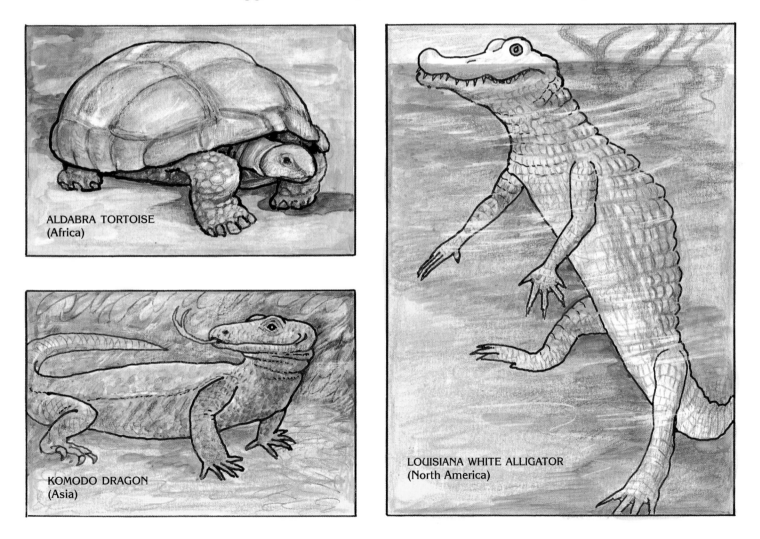

ALDABRA TORTOISE
(Africa)

KOMODO DRAGON
(Asia)

LOUISIANA WHITE ALLIGATOR
(North America)

a giant lizard, and my favorite—a rare white alligator, floating in water.

The Children's Zoo was packed with things to see and do.
There were animals to pet and touch, a dovecote,
and a Mouse House baked in the zoo.
Friendly keepers and docents answered our questions,
and we even saw babies in the nursery.

GREAT HORNED OWL
(North/South
America)

PORCUPINE
(North America)

BURROWING OWL
(North/South America)

BABY GIANT ANTEATER
(South America)

MOUSE HOUSE

SAN DIEGO MOUSE
(North America)

WHITE'S TREE FROG
(Australia)

BELL AVENUE SCHOOL

RECIPE FOR A MOUSE HOUSE

6 cups water   ½ cup sugar
2 tbsp. yeast   2 tbsp. salt
12 cups flour   ¾ cup shortening

Mix all ingredients together. Knead. Let rise,
punch down, let rise again. Bake 15 minutes at 425°F,
one hour at 325°F. For a smaller loaf, reduce measurements
by one quarter.

DOVE
(worldwide)

NURSERY

SHHH...
BABIES
SLEEPING

LEOPARD BABY
(Africa)

BOA CONSTRICTOR
(South America)

SHEEP
(worldwide)

NUBIAN GOAT
(worldwide)

RABBIT
(worldwide)

POTBELLIED PIG
(Vietnam)

31

While we were grazing in the bookstore, the clock chimed.
It was closing time and we had not seen everything yet.
My cousin promised we would come back next time I visit.
And to think I almost stayed home!

THE WORLD

NEW WORLD   OLD WORLD

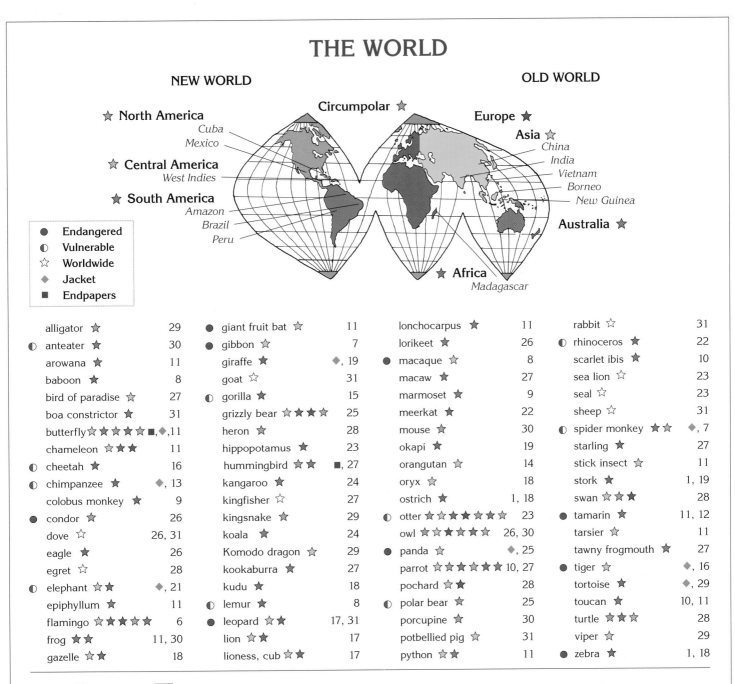

☆ North America
Cuba
Mexico

Circumpolar ★

Europe ★

Asia ☆

☆ Central America
West Indies

China
India
Vietnam
Borneo
New Guinea

☆ South America
Amazon
Brazil
Peru

Australia ★

● Endangered
◐ Vulnerable
☆ Worldwide
◆ Jacket
■ Endpapers

★ Africa
Madagascar

	alligator ★	29	● giant fruit bat ☆	11	lonchocarpus ★	11	rabbit ☆	31
◐	anteater ★	30	● gibbon ☆	7	lorikeet ★	26	◐ rhinoceros ★	22
	arowana ★	11	giraffe ★ ◆, 19		● macaque ☆	8	scarlet ibis ★	10
	baboon ★	8	goat ☆	31	macaw ★	27	sea lion ☆	23
	bird of paradise ☆	27	◐ gorilla ★	15	marmoset ★	9	seal ☆	23
	boa constrictor ★	31	grizzly bear ☆ ★ ★ ☆	25	meerkat ★	22	sheep ☆	31
	butterfly ☆ ★ ★ ☆ ■,◆,11		heron ☆	28	mouse ☆	30	◐ spider monkey ★ ★ ◆, 7
	chameleon ☆ ★ ★	11	hippopotamus ★	23	okapi ★	19	starling ★	27
◐	cheetah ★	16	hummingbird ★ ★ ■, 27		orangutan ☆	14	stick insect ☆	11
◐	chimpanzee ★ ◆, 13		kangaroo ★	24	oryx ☆	18	stork ★	1, 19
	colobus monkey ★	9	kingfisher ☆	27	ostrich ★	1, 18	swan ☆ ☆ ★	28
●	condor ☆	26	kingsnake ★	29	◐ otter ☆ ☆ ★ ★ ★ ☆	23	● tamarin ★	11, 12
	dove ☆	26, 31	koala ★	24	owl ☆ ★ ★ ★ ★ ☆	26, 30	tarsier ☆	11
	eagle ★	26	Komodo dragon ☆	29	● panda ☆ ◆, 25		tawny frogmouth ★	27
	egret ☆	28	kookaburra ★	27	parrot ☆ ★ ★ ★ ★ 10, 27		● tiger ☆ ◆, 16
◐	elephant ☆ ★ ◆, 21		kudu ★	18	pochard ☆ ★	28	tortoise ◆, 29
	epiphyllum ★	11	◐ lemur ★	8	◐ polar bear ★	25	toucan ★	10, 11
	flamingo ☆ ★ ★ ★	6	● leopard ☆ ★	17, 31	porcupine ☆	30	turtle ★ ★ ☆	28
	frog ★ ★	11, 30	lion ☆ ★	17	potbellied pig ☆	31	viper ☆	29
	gazelle ☆ ★	18	lioness, cub ☆ ★	17	python ☆ ★	11	● zebra ★	1, 18

For a long time, human beings have been the most dangerous species on the planet. Knowingly, or without thinking, they have destroyed, endangered, polluted, and changed the air, water, and life on earth.

Now there is hope. Many concerned people are working to reverse the damage done. In groups or alone, they protect animals, defend indigenous peoples, plant trees, save, recycle, and refuse to pollute.

Even zoos are changing their old ways. Zoos have become sanctuaries— safe conservation parks where animals are born, protected, and given a chance to survive.

Some say that animals do not belong in captivity. But without caring zoos, more wildlife would be at risk, and we would lose the privilege of seeing the animals. Zoos need our support. Together we can all create a miracle— to help animals stay alive and make the world a better place.

CRIMSON TOPAZ
(South America)

LARGE
TREE NYMPH
(Asia)

CAIRNS
BIRDWING
(New Guinea
to Australia)

BLUE
MORPHO
(South
America)

TIGER
SWALLOWTAIL
(North America)

BEE
HUMMINGBIRD
(Cuba)

LODDIGE'S
RAQUET-TAIL
(Peru)

TIGER PIERID
(Central/South America ·
Mexico · West Indies)

CRAMER'S MESENE
(Central/South
America)